Unit 5

HOUGHTON MIFFLIN HARCOURT
School Publishers

Contents

mustangs

by Meish Goldish

This is a herd of mustangs. This herd is running hard. Each horse can move fast! The herd thunders across the land.

Mustangs are wild animals. Some mustangs roam in herds on open land in the West. Mustangs can be quite wild. They leap and kick. Each mustang is quick and strong. Mustangs act up more than most other kinds of horses.

Wild mustangs first roamed open plains a long, long time ago. Spanish explorers had tame horses when they came to our land. Some Spanish horses escaped and became wild. Those horses became the first wild mustangs.

Trained mustangs make fine riding horses. Mustangs run fast and are quite strong. Ranch hands ride mustangs on the job. These horses help them keep track of other animals on the ranch.

This mustang herd has stopped by a river. These horses drink lots of water. Horses need to drink, just like people. Mustangs travel in the hot sun. On hot days, there is nothing like cool drinks!

In the old West, ranchers rode mustangs. Ranchers led large herds of animals on long trips. Some mustangs led the herd. Other mustangs stayed on each side of the herd. Other mustangs traveled behind the herd.

Mustangs would work hard on long trips. Along the way, an animal might try to run away. Men on mustangs went after that animal. Those men and mustangs made it get back with the rest of the herd. Nothing got past those fast mustangs!

In times past, mustangs helped with work. Today, mustangs still help. People on ranches and farms ride these tame horses across the land. Other mustangs are still wild. These horses run free in herds. Tame or wild, there is nothing quite like mustangs!

Time to Move

by Mae Meriva

illustrated by Andrea Shine

Burt gazed out his window. In three
days, his family would move. Burt did
not wish to leave his home. Burt was sad.

Mom came in and sat on the bed with Burt. Burt did not stir. Mom placed her hand on his arm.

"It's hard to move," Mom sighed.

"It hurts a lot," Burt blurted out. "I will miss this home."

Burt began to cry. He wiped his wet
face on his shirt sleeve. At first, Mom
said nothing. Then she turned to Burt.

"What will you miss most about this
home?" she asked.

"I will show you," Burt said.

Burt turned to his window. "I like
that birch tree in our yard," Burt sighed.
"Look at its third branch. There is a nest
with a bird in it. Each day, I see that
bird. I like how it sings and chirps."

Mom turned to Burt. "I can see why you will miss that," she said.

"Look closer," Burt added. "That nest has eggs in it. Those eggs will hatch soon. I will miss the chicks as well."

The next day, Burt gazed out his
window. He saw the birch tree in the
yard. Burt burst into a happy cheer.

"Mom!" Burt cried. "Those bird eggs
hatched! Three baby chicks are in that
nest. You must see them!"

"Let's have a birthday party!" Mom
cried. "After all, today is the birthday for
those birds!"

Burt clapped his hands. He and Mom
danced and whirled.

"Happy birthday, birds!" Burt sang.

Burt felt better. He helped Mom pack his shirts.

"Those birds will move one day," Mom said. "They will need more space."

"Maybe they will find a place in our new yard!" Burt added.

What's That?

by Meish Goldish
illustrated by Monique Passicot

Pam had a party at her home. Jason, Billy, and Jen came.

"Let's play a game," Pam cried.

"Let's play 'What's That?'" Jason cried.

Pam, Jason, Billy, and Jen sat on the floor. Pam began the game.

"What are seven days that are not strong?" Pam asked.

Billy raised his hand. "I know!" he cried. "A weak week!"

"Right!" Pam cried. "Now it's your turn. Make up a joke."

Billy thought for a moment. Then he smiled at his pals.

"I've got it," Billy cried. "What happens when you shake hands with hot dogs?" Billy smiled again and waited.

The players sat silent for a moment. Then Jen raised her hand.

"I know!" she cried. "You meet meat."

Jen snapped her fingers. "This is hard but funny," she cried. "What cards and letters are not for girls?"

Jason jumped up. "I think I know!" he cried. "Male mail."

"That's correct, Jason!" Jen cried. "Now you give it a try."

Jason had to make up a joke. He
stepped toward the window. "I must
pace back and forth when I think,"
he explained.

Soon, Jason had a joke. "Why do
boats need eyes?" he asked.

"To see the sea!" Pam cried.

"We each got one right. This game ends in a tie," Pam said.

"No!" Jason cried. "Let's play one more time to get a winner."

"Who will think up the joke?" Jen asked. "That person will not get to win. Let's think about this."

Just then, Mister Baker came in.

"Dad, please make up a joke for our game, 'What's That?'" Pam asked.

Mister Baker came up with a joke. "What fur is on rabbits?" he asked.

"Hare hair!" everyone yelled at the same time.

"Yes, I win!" Pam cried. "I got two jokes right."

"But I got two, too," Jason cried.

"And we got up to two, too," Billy and Jen cried. "That's funny!"

Pam, Jason, Billy, and Jen giggled for a long, long time.

Get Smarter!

by Beth Dinn

Be smart. Be smarter. Be the smartest
you can be! Start by reading these quiz
pages and train your brain.

Which is longer, five feet or one yard? Think hard and don't rush. Five feet is sixty inches long. One yard is thirty-six inches long. So five feet is much, much longer! That's smart thinking!

What's higher, a pile of ten nickels or ten dimes? Place them side by side. The nickel pile is higher. Nickels are thicker than dimes. Yet dimes can get you twice as much stuff in stores!

What's older, a dam or a foal? Both
dams and foals are horses. A foal is a
baby horse. A dam is its mother. So that
means dams must be older than foals.
Don't you feel much smarter?

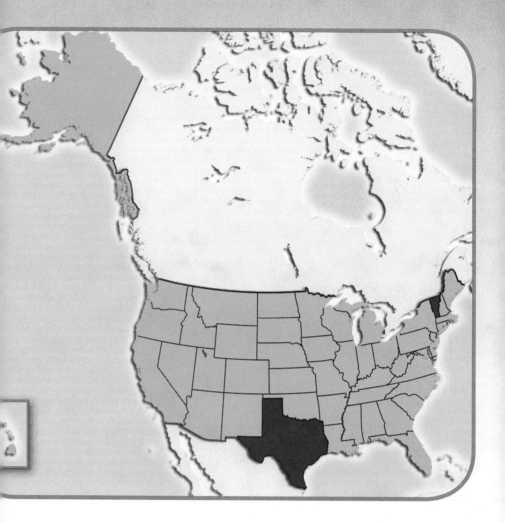

Which is a bigger state, Texas or Vermont? Texas is much bigger. It is about thirty times bigger in size than Vermont. In fact, Texas is the second biggest state in our land.

This quiz is about the sea: Which is wider, the floor in your home or in the sea? The sea floor is miles and miles and miles wide. The floor in your home is not that wide!

What's the longest fish in the sea?
It's the whale shark. Whale sharks are
sharks, not whales. Whale sharks can be
more than forty feet long. That's as long
as a long bus!

What's the longest of all the words you can use? "Smiles"! "Smiles" is the longest. There's a "mile" between the first and last letter. That's far!

Quizzes solved! You are on your way toward being smarter.

Fraidy Cat

by Bobbie N. Zaide
illustrated by Sandy Kossin

My cat Fraidy is mostly playful. She
likes to run and leap all over. At times,
though, she can make big problems.
That's what happened last week.

The day began. Mom made toast. I began to put jam on my toast. One drop of jam dripped off my plate. Sadly, it landed on Fraidy. That jam would lead to a big problem!

I leaned down quickly to help Fraidy.
I tried wiping that sticky jam off her fur.
Yet Fraidy would not let me. She had
another idea. Suddenly she leaped right
out the open kitchen window!

Fraidy can be such a handful of
problems! Mom and I made a speedy
dash out of the house to catch that cat.
At first we didn't see her. Then she cried
softly. Fraidy had run up a tree! She sat
safely on a high branch.

"Fraidy, kindly get down right now,"
I said sweetly. "Fraidy, get down."

Fraidy didn't move. I cried to her
again, but she stayed firmly in place.
She had a needy look on her face.

"Mom," I sighed, "Fraidy is afraid."

"I've got an idea," Mom said.

She went back inside. Then she came back with a plateful of cat food. "This may get her down," Mom told me. "Come and get it, Fraidy! It is cat food, Fraidy!" Mom cried in a hopeful tone.

Mom and I both waited. We just knew that Fraidy would gladly run to us. That didn't happen, though. Fraidy sat with that same painful look on her face.

"There is just one more thing that we can try," Mom suggested.

Mom told Dad about Fraidy. Dad had
a long ladder on his truck that he used
when he painted the house. Dad came
swiftly. He got that cat down in no time.

Like I told you, at times Fraidy can
make big problems!

Bugs in *Action*

by Ben Sorare
illustrated by John Hovell

It was the last day of bug school. The large class of bugs lined up in rows. Each creature felt quite happy. At last, Doc Bug got up to speak.

"Class," Doc Bug began, "you are
mature creatures at last. You are starting
life on your own. You will see plenty
of action. I am hopeful that you will
be fine. Living in nature can be hard,
though. Hard but fun."

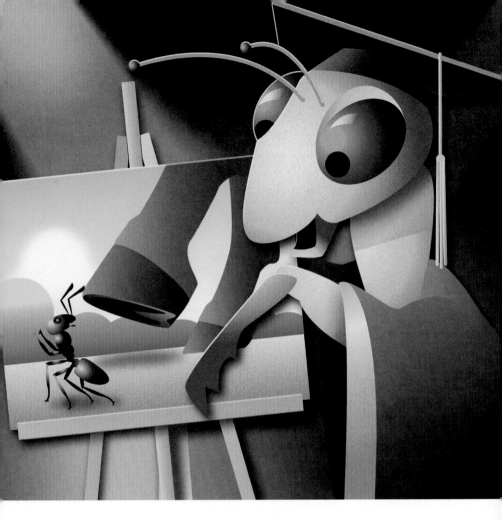

Ant spoke up. "What is hard about living in nature?" Ant asked.

Doc Bug held up some pictures. "See this?" Doc Bug asked. "An ant is small, while other animals are huge. Don't get stepped on. Stay in motion."

Next, Ladybug had a question. "If I
fly, will I fracture my shell?" Ladybug
asked. "Will I, Doc?"

"No," Doc Bug said. "When you are
in motion, don't get too close to trees or
rocks. Then, you will be safe."

"I never knew that," Ladybug sighed.

Doc Bug held up some more pictures.
"Stay close to small plants and grass.
That will keep your shell safe. If you fly
by a garden, you can get a snack, too."

"Nice idea," Ladybug agreed.

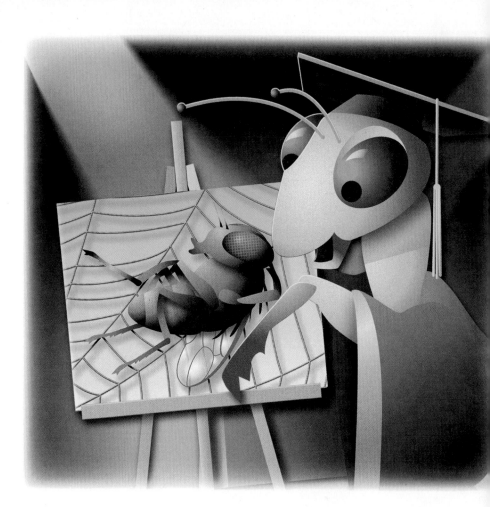

Fly spoke up next. "Can you mention how I can stay safe?" Fly asked.

Doc Bug changed pictures yet again. "Spiders like to capture flies. Spiders spin sticky webs. Flies get stuck on them," Doc Bug explained.

"Don't go near any sticky webs!"
Doc Bug cried.

"That seems like a fine idea," Fly
agreed. "I never knew that living in
nature was so hard."

"It's fun if you stay safe," Doc said.

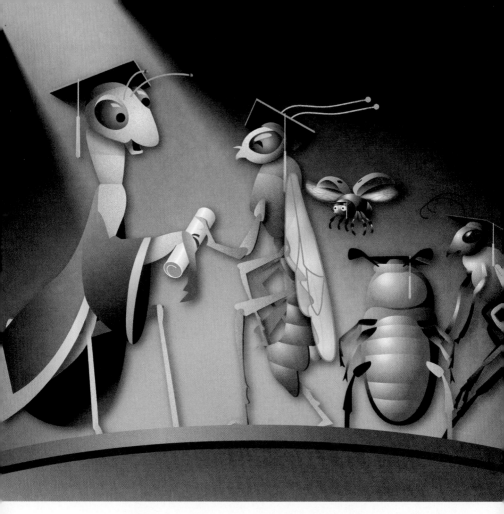

Doc Bug smiled at the class of bugs. "You are the future of our bug nation," Doc Bug cried. "Don't forget that bugs help nature a lot. My lecture is over. Now go out and live!"

So they did!

The Unreal Party

by Bo Bayom
illustrated by Kristen Goeters

Ann was planning her first party. "It will be unreal!" she cried.

Ann needed her party to be perfect. "I can't overlook a thing," she told herself.

Ann made a list of pals to invite. She rechecked her list three times.

"We can help you plan this party," her older brothers told her.

"No, thanks," Ann said. "I can do it myself. It will be an unreal party, and it will be all mine!"

Ann began making cards to send to
her pals. She told them the day and time
for her party. Ann printed slowly. She
didn't misspell any words.

"May we help?" her brothers asked.

"Please go away," Ann sighed.
"Thanks, but no thanks."

Next, Ann planned food for her party. Which treats can be eaten cold? Which ill Mom and Dad need to reheat? Ann le her list.

can't forget a thing," Ann reminded "This party will be unreal!"

That week, Ann got red and green
paper streamers for her party. She taped
them up. Three streamers fell. Her
brothers tried to retape them.

"I'll retape them," Ann said. "I must
not leave a thing unfinished."

At last, it was party day. Ann was
dressed up. Ann waited for her pals. She
unlocked the door. Mom preheated the
kitchen stove.

Ann, Dad, and Mom waited and
waited. No one came! Did everyone
lost the card she had sent?

Ann phoned her best pal, Lexy. "Why are you not at my party, Lexy?" Ann asked her. "It is party time."

"What on earth do you mean?" Lexy replied. "I never got a card."

"Oh, no!" Ann cried. "I forgot to mail my cards. I never sent them!"

Ann felt so unhappy. She had
forgotten something huge. "Now I must
rethink my party," she sighed.

"Well, this party really was unreal,"
her brothers joked. "We'll help you make
the next party a real good time."

Knick and Knack

by Beth Dinn
illustrated by Jon Goodell

Knick and Knack are twin lambs. The brothers live with other Bighorn sheep on this high rocky cliff.

Knick and Knack loved to climb all over the place. Knick, Knack, and Mom had fun climbing cliffs.

One day Knick was climbing along
a cliff. He jumped away as a big rock
began to roll. Down it went!

"Look at that!" yelled Knack. "See
that deep hole where that rock used to be?
Maybe it's a cave."

"Maybe we can go right in," added
Knick. "Can we explore it?"

"Yes, I'll go in with you," said Mom.
"This is High Cliff Cave. I used to climb
and explore High Cliff Cave with my dad.
We came here many times."

Mom went into High Cliff Cave. Knick
and Knack followed Mom. Knick and
Knack did not know what to expect.

The dim light that came into High
Cliff Cave helped them see. Inside, they
sat and rested on the damp earth.

Suddenly, Knick jumped up. "Look at those paintings," exclaimed Knick.

"Where?" asked Knack.

"Just behind you!" cried Knick.

Knack turned and was surprised. Knack saw a lot of paintings.

Mom smiled at her lambs' surprise.
Knick and Knack saw paintings of
Bighorn sheep and lambs climbing on
a cliff. There was writing under each
painting.

Knick and Knack were amazed, but
Mom was not. She just gazed at them.

"Did you know that these paintings were in this cave?" asked Knick.

"I did know," said Mom.

"How did you know?" asked Knack.

"Because I painted those paintings myself, and my dad wrote the writing," Mom said.

"Can we make paintings of Bighorn sheep and lambs?" asked Knick.

"Yes, can we?" asked Knack.

"You can," agreed Mom. "We will find a place in this cave that is just right for you. You can paint and I will help with the writing."

Knick and Knack loved that plan. Soon Knick and Knack were making their own cave paintings.

A Spring Walk

by Meish Goldish

Which season is best? Many people think it is spring. What makes them feel that way? It's because of all that spring has to offer.

Walk through a park in spring. Nice things can be seen. New leaves grow on plants and trees. These young leaves are called buds. In a short time, these small leaf buds will grow larger.

Lawns turn green in spring. Playful
animals can be seen running all over.
Dogs chase balls that are tossed to them.
Frogs hop on and off small logs. Birds
chirp and call. It's their way of talking!

Young kids and grownups alike fly
kites in the spring. Large and small kites
are launched in happy breezes. Kites of
all shapes and sizes dance across the sky.
Some kites will stand tall and some kites
will dip down and fall.

   Spring is also the time when baseball
season begins. You can almost always
find ball games going on in the park.
Baseball games draw many fans. It's
funny how such a small ball can cause
such big excitement!

Is there a nicer time for walking than
spring? Walk in winter, and it's too cold.
You might slip and fall on the snow or
ice. Most trees have no leaves on them in
winter. Who wants that?

You can get chilly walking in fall.
Cold winds may blow at your back.

Summer can often be far too hot for
walking. The blazing sun might slow
your walk to a crawl. Who wants that?

Next spring, take long, peaceful walks.
See trees and plants that you never saw
before. Watch baseball games. See tall
kites float in the sky. Do all of it, just
because it's spring!

The Softball Game

by Morris Ayin
illustrated by Elizabeth Allen

It is fall. Trees in the park have yellow and red leaves. Two teams play softball under these trees.

Paul is at bat for the Sliders. It is the last inning in this game with the Hawks.

The score is Sliders 2, Hawks 2. "Let's go, Paul!" Coach called. "We can win this game with just one more run!"

The pitcher for the Hawks tossed the softball. Paul wanted to hit a home run. He swung hard but missed the ball.

"Strike!" the umpire called.

Paul clenched his jaw. He wanted to launch that softball over the wall!

The pitcher tossed the ball. Paul swung hard but he missed it. This time, he began to fall. A small but funny feeling ran down his arm. Coach saw Paul fall on the base.

Coach ran over to talk to Paul.

"Go now and let Nurse Donna see this arm," Coach ordered.

Paul walked over to Nurse Donna. She felt his arm. She saw that it was okay.

"No more playing today," she said. "Just watch, Paul. Just watch."

The Sliders had no player to replace Paul. "That means we win this game!" the Hawks cried. The happy Hawks tossed Hawk caps all over.

"Not so fast!" Paul cried. "My sister Shawna can play for me. Shawna plays well and she can hit."

"No! Shawna is too young! She can't play!" the Hawks yelled.

Coach talked with the umpire. She looked in her rule book. "There is no law about age," the umpire called. "So Shawna can play after all."

Shawna walked to home plate.

"We can win this game with just one more run!" Coach called to Shawna.

Shawna wanted to win for Paul. The pitcher for the Hawks tossed the softball. Shawna swung hard.

Whack! The softball sailed through
the air. Shawna watched it as she ran.
Her ball sailed over the wall. Shawna
had hit a home run! She slid into home
plate. Then Shawna jumped back up!

The winning Sliders tossed caps all
over. "My small sister can do big things!"
Paul called.

Word Lists

Accompanies
Penguin Chick

Mustangs

page 1

Decodable Words
Target Skill: *r-controlled vowel er*
explorers, herd, herds, thunders

Words Using Previously Taught Skills
act, after, ago, along, and, animal,
animals, back, be, became, by, came,
can, cool, days, drink, drinks, each,
escaped, farms, fast, fine, free, get, got,
had, hands, hard, has, help, helped,
horse, horses, hot, in, is, job, just, keep,
kick, kinds, land, large, leap, led, like,
long, lots, made, make, men, might,
more, most, mustang, mustangs, need,
old, on, open, past, plains, quick, quite,
ranch, ranches, rest, ride, riding, river,
roam, roamed, rode, run, running, side,
Spanish, stayed, still, stopped, strong,
sun, tame, than, that, them, these, this,
those, time, times, track, trained, travel,
traveled, trips, try, up, way, went, West,
when, wild

High-Frequency Words
New
across, move, nothing

Previously Taught
a, are, away, first, of, other,
our, people, some, the,
there, they, to, today, water,
work

Time to Move

page 9

Decodable Words
Target Skill: *r-controlled vowels ir, ur*
birch, bird, birds, birthday, blurted,
burst, Burt, chirps, first, hurts, shirt,
shirts, stir, third, turned, whirled

Target Skill: *r-controlled vowel er*
after, better, closer, her

Words Using Previously Taught Skills
added, and, arm, asked, at, baby,
bed, began, branch, came, can, cheer,
chicks, cried, cry, danced, day, days,
did, each, eggs, face, family, felt, find,
for, gazed, hand, happy, hard, has,
hatch, hatched, he, helped, his, home,
I, in, into, is, it, it's, its, leave, let's,
like, lot, maybe, miss, Mom, more,
most, move, must, need, nest, next,
not, on, pack, party, place, placed,
sad, sang, sat, see, she, show, sighed,
sings, sleeve, space, that, them, then,
this, those, three, tree, well, wet, will,
window, wiped, wish, with, yard

High-Frequency Words
New
move, nothing

Previously Taught
a, about, all, are, have, how,
laughed, look, new, one,
our, out, said, saw, soon,
the, there, they, to, today,
was, what, why, would, you

What's That?

page 17

Decodable Words
Target Skill: *Homophones*
eye/I, hair/hare, know/no, mail/male, meat/meet, sea/see, to/too/two, weak/week

Words Using Previously Taught Skills
an, and, asked, at, back, Baker, began, Billy, boats, but, came, cards, correct, cried, Dad, days, dogs, each, ends, explained, fingers, for, forth, funny, fur, game, get, giggled, girls, got, had, hand, hands, happens, hard, he, her, his, home, hot, I've, is, it, it's, Jason, Jen, joke, jokes, jumped, just, let's, letters, long, make, Mister, moment, more, must, need, not, on, pace, pals, Pam, party, person, play, players, please, rabbits, raised, raised, right, same, sat, seven, shake, silent, smiled, snapped, stepped, strong, that, that's, then, think, this, tie, time, try, turn, up, waited, we, when, why, will, win, window, winner, with, yelled, yes

High-Frequency Words
New
floor, toward, what's

Previously Taught
a, about, again, are, do, everyone, eyes, give, now, one, our, said, soon, the, thought, to, too, two, what, who, you, your

Get Smarter! page 25

Decodable Words

Target Skill: *Base Words and -er, -est, including doubling of final consonant*
bigger, biggest, higher, longer, longest, smarter, smartest, thicker, wider

Words Using Previously Taught Skills

and, baby, be, between, both, brain, bus, by, can, dam, dams, dimes, don't, fact, far, feel, feet, first, fish, five, foal, foals, forty, get, hard, home, horse, horses, in, inches, is, it, it's, its, land, last, letter, long, means, mile, miles, more, much, must, nickel, nickels, not, older, or, pages, pile, place, quiz, quizzes, reading, rush, sea, shark, sharks, side, sixty, size, smart, smiles, so, solved, start, state, stores, stuff, ten, Texas, than, that, that's, them, these, think, thinking, thirty, thirty-six, this, times, train, twice, use, Vermont, way, whale, whales, which, wide, yard, yet

High-Frequency Words

New
floor, toward, what's

Previously Taught
all, nearly, of, second, the, words, you

Fraidy Cat

page 33

Decodable Words
Target Skill: *Suffixes -y, -ly, -ful*
Fraidy, firmly, gladly, handful, hopeful, kindly, mostly, needy, painful, plateful, playful, quickly, sadly, safely, softly, speedy, sticky, suddenly, sweetly, swiftly

Words Using Previously Taught Skills
afraid, an, and, at, back, be, began, big, both, branch, but, came, can, cat, catch, cried, Dad , dash, day, didn't, dripped, drop, face, first, food, fur, get, got, had, happen, happened, he, help, her, high, his, hoped, I, I've, idea, in, inside, is, it, jam, just, kitchen, ladder, landed, last, lead, leaned, leap, leaped, let, like, likes, long, made, make, may, me, Mom, more, my, no, not, on, open, over, painted, place, plate, problem, problems, right, run, same, sat, see, she, sighed, started, stayed, such, suggested, that, that's, then, thing, this, time, times, toast, told, tone, tree, tried, truck, try, up, us, used, waited, we, week, went, when, window, wiping, with, yet

High-Frequency Words
New
idea, knew, though

Previously Taught
a, about, again, all, another, come, down, house, look, move, now, of, off, one, out, outside, put, said, the, there, to, what, would, you

85

Bugs in Action

page 41

Decodable Words
Target Skill: *Common syllables -tion, -ture*

action, capture, creature, creatures, fracture, future, lecture, mature, mention, motion, nation, nature, question

Target Skill: *Suffixes -y, -ly, -ful*
hopeful, sticky

Words Using Previously Taught Skills
agreed, am, an, and, animals, Ant, asked, at, be, began, bug, bugs, but, by, can, class, close, cried, day, did, Doc, don't, each, explained, felt, fine, flies, fly, forget, fun, garden, get, go, got, grass, had, happy, hard, held, help, how, huge, I, if, in, is, it, it's, keep, Ladybug, large, last, life, like, lined, live, living, lot, my, never, next, nice, no, on, or, over, own, plants, plenty, quite, rocks, rows, safe, school, see, seems, shell, sighed, small, smiled, snack, so, speak, spiders, spin, spoke, starting, stay, stepped, stuck, that, them, then, this, trees, up, webs, when, while, will, yet

High-Frequency Words
New
idea, knew, though

Previously Taught
a, about, again, another, any, are, near, now, of, other, our, out, pictures, said, some, the, they, to, too, was, what, you, your

The Unreal Party

page 49

Decodable Words

Target Skill: *Prefixes re-, un-, over-,
pre-, mis-*

misread, misspell, overlook, preheated,
rechecked, reheat, reminded, replied,
retape, rethink, unfinished, unhappy,
unlocked, unreal

Words Using Previously Taught Skills

an, and, Ann, asked, at, be, began,
best, but, came, can, can't, card, cards,
cold, cried, Dad, day, didn't, dressed,
eaten, fell, felt, first, for, forget, forgot,
forgotten, go, got, green, had, help,
her, herself, huge, I, I'll, invite, it, joked,
kitchen, last, leave, Lexy, list, made,
mail, make, making, may, mean, mine,
Mom, must, my, myself, need, needed,
never, next, no, not, oh, older, pals,
paper, party, perfect, phoned, plan,
planned, planning, please, printed,
real, really, red, send, sent, she, sighed,
slowly, so, stove, streamers, taped,
thanks, that, them, thing, this, three,
time, times, told, treats, tried, up,
waited, we, we'll, week, well, which,
why, will

High-Frequency Words

New

away, brothers, earth

Previously Taught

a, all, any, are, do, door,
everyone, food, good, now,
of, one, said, something,
to, was, words, you

87

Knick and Knack

page 57

Decodable Words
Target Skill: *Silent consonants gh, w(r), k(n), (m)b*
climb, climbing, high, Knack, Knick, lambs, lambs', light, right, wrote

Words Using Previously Taught Skills
added, agreed, along, amazed, and, as, asked, at, be, began, behind, big, Bighorn, but, came, can, cave, cliff, cliffs, cried, dad, damp, day, deep, did, dim, down, each, exclaimed, expect, explore, find, followed, fun, gazed, go, had, he, helped, her, hole, how, I'll, in, inside, it, it's, jumped, just, live, lot, make, making, maybe, Mom, my, myself, not, on, over, own, paint, painted, paintings, place, plan, rested, rock, rocky, roll, sat, see, she, sheep, smiled, suddenly, surprise, surprised, that, them, these, this, those, times, turned, twin, under, up, used, we, went, will, with, writing, yelled, yes

High-Frequency Words
New
away, brothers, earth

Previously Taught
a, all, are, because, here, into, know, look, loved, many, of, one, other, said, saw, soon, the, their, there, they, to, was, were, what, where, you

A Spring Walk
page 65

Decodable Words
Target Skill: *Spellings for /aw/: au, aw;*
al; o; a
all, almost, also, always, ball, balls,
baseball, call, called, cause, crawl, draw,
fall, launched, lawns, logs, long, off,
offer, often, saw, small, talking, tall,
tossed, walk, walking, walks

Words Using Previously Taught Skills
across, alike, and, animals, back, be,
because, before, begins, best, big, birds,
blazing, blow, breezes, buds, can, chase,
chilly, chirp, cold, dance, dip, dogs,
down, excitement, fans, far, feel, find,
float, fly, for, frogs, funny, games, get,
going, green, grow, grownups, happy,
has, hop, hot, ice, in, is, it, it's, just,
kids, kites, large, larger, leaf, makes,
many, may, might, most, never, next,
nice, nicer, no, on, over, park, peaceful,
plants, playful, running, season, see,
seen, shapes, short, sizes, sky, slip, slow,
snow, spring, stand, such, summer, sun,
take, than, that, them, these, things,
think, time, trees, turn, wants, watch,
way, when, which, will, winds, winter

High-Frequency Words
New
leaves, through, young

Previously Taught
a, are, do, have, how, new,
of, people, some, the, their,
there, to, too, what, who,
you, your

89

The Softball Game
page 73

Decodable Words
Target Skill: *Spellings for /aw/: au, aw; al; o; a*
all, ball, called, fall, Hawks, jaw, launch, law, Paul, saw, Shawna, small, softball, talk, talked, tossed, walked, wall, watch, watched

Words Using Previously Taught Skills
after, age, and, arm, as, at, back, base, bat, began, big, but, can, can't, caps, clenched, Coach, cried, Donna, fast, feeling, felt, for, funny, game, go, had, happy, hard, he, his, hit, home, in, inning, into, is, it, jumped, just, last, let, let's, me, means, missed, more, my, no, not, Nurse, okay, ordered, over, park, pitcher, plate, play, player, playing, plays, ran, red, replace, rule, run, sailed, score, see, she, sister, slid, Sliders, so, strike, swung, teams, that, these, things, this, time, trees, umpire, under, up, wanted, we, well, whack, win, winning, with, yelled, yellow

High-Frequency Words
New
leaves, through, young

Previously Taught
a, about, air, book, do, down, have, look, now, one, said, the, there, to, today, too, two, was